THE COVID-19 PANDEMIC

THE COVID-19 VIRUS

by Walt K. Moon

BrightPoint Press

San Diego, CA

BrightPoint Press

© 2021 BrightPoint Press
an imprint of ReferencePoint Press, Inc.
Printed in the United States

For more information, contact:
BrightPoint Press
PO Box 27779
San Diego, CA 92198
www.BrightPointPress.com

LIBRARY OF CONGRESS CATALOGING-IN-PUBLICATION DATA

Names: Moon, Walt K., author.
Title: The COVID-19 virus / by Walt K. Moon.
Description: San Diego, CA : BrightPoint Press, [2021] | Series: The COVID-19 pandemic | Includes bibliographical references and index. | Audience: Grades 7-9
Identifiers: LCCN 2020047455 (print) | LCCN 2020047456 (eBook) | ISBN 9781678200565 (hardcover) | ISBN 9781678200572 (eBook)
Subjects: LCSH: COVID-19 (Disease)--Juvenile literature.
Classification: LCC RA644.C67 M67 2021 (print) | LCC RA644.C67 (eBook) | DDC 614.5/92414--dc23
LC record available at https://lccn.loc.gov/2020047455
LC eBook record available at https://lccn.loc.gov/2020047456

CONTENTS

AT A GLANCE

- The COVID-19 pandemic spread around the world in 2020. This disease is caused by a virus called SARS-CoV-2.

- SARS-CoV-2 belongs to a family of viruses called coronaviruses.

- SARS-CoV-2 invades healthy human cells. It forces cells to produce copies of the virus. After killing cells, new copies of the virus spread to other cells, and the process repeats.

- For some people, COVID-19 causes mild symptoms or even no symptoms. For others, the disease is deadly.

- The virus harms cells in the respiratory system, damaging the lungs and making breathing difficult.

- The virus spreads through droplets that leave the mouth and nose when infected people cough, sneeze, speak, or sing. If others breathe in these droplets, they can get infected.

- People can practice social distancing, wear masks, and wash their hands to stay safe. These steps slow the spread of the virus.

- During the pandemic, scientists worked quickly on a vaccine. A vaccine could save lives and bring the pandemic to an end.

FROM WUHAN TO THE WORLD

The city of Wuhan is found in central China, 400 miles (640 km) west of the Pacific coast. With a population of 11 million, it has more people than New York City. It is the capital of Hubei Province.

Like many Chinese cities, Wuhan has wet markets. They are an important part of everyday life in China. Sellers at these busy

The first known case of COVID-19 was discovered in Wuhan, China.

outdoor markets offer fresh seafood, meat, fruits, and vegetables. Some markets also sell live animals.

Wet markets, which sell perishable food items, are common throughout China.

In December 2019, people in Wuhan started getting sick with pneumonia. This condition affects the lungs and makes it difficult to breathe. Many of the people had been to the same wet market in Wuhan.

Scientists studied these sick people. They soon discovered that an unknown virus had caused the pneumonia. It was similar to an earlier virus called SARS-CoV. Researchers later named this new virus SARS-CoV-2. They called the disease it caused COVID-19.

Diseases can spread from animals to humans. Scientists said it was unlikely this happened at the market. The earliest cases were not connected to the market. But the market was where the disease first began to spread widely from person to person.

A NEW OUTBREAK

Wuhan became the center of the COVID-19 outbreak. The virus spread to thousands of people in the area. On January 11,

2020, China reported the first death from COVID-19. It was a man who had been a regular customer at the wet market. On January 23, China blocked travel into and out of Wuhan.

However, the virus had already reached other countries. The first case in the United States was found on January 21. It was a man from Washington State. He had recently visited family in Wuhan.

The global numbers of cases and deaths continued to rise. By February 1, there were more than 10,000 cases and 250 deaths. The virus kept spreading through

COVID-19 quickly spread around the world in early 2020.

the year. By December, there were more

than 63 million cases. COVID-19 had killed

almost 1.5 million people. A virus far too tiny

to be seen by the human eye had changed

the world forever.

CHAPTER ONE

WHAT IS A CORONAVIRUS?

Viruses are tiny particles with one purpose: to make copies of themselves. They cannot do this alone. A virus must first **invade** a living cell. Then it uses the cell to **reproduce**. The cell fills with copies of the virus, which kills the cell. The new viruses invade other cells, and the

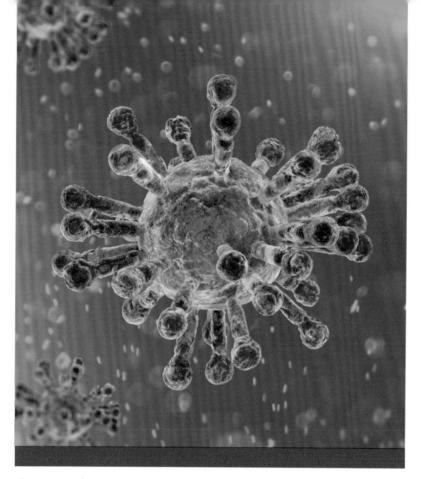

Coronaviruses such as SARS-CoV-2 have many spikes.

process repeats. Many cells die. This is how viruses make people sick.

A virus has two basic parts. The first is genetic material. It may be RNA

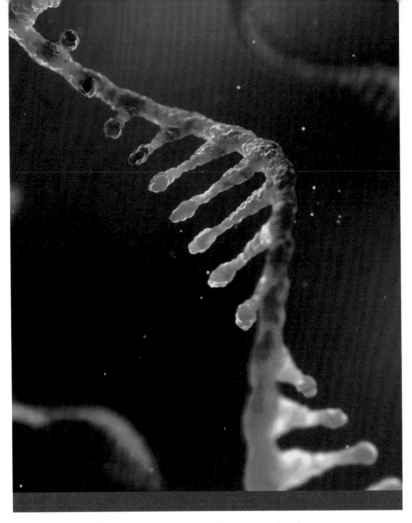

A strand of RNA is shaped like a spiral.

or DNA. These are chemicals that contain

instructions for building a cell or a virus. For

example, a person's height and eye color

are represented in his or her DNA. Cells

copy their own genetic material to create

new cells. Viruses take over this ability

to instead make copies of themselves.

The second part of the virus is an outer

shell of **proteins**. It protects the genetic

material inside.

Viruses attack cells in specific areas.

Viruses that cause the common cold

strike the upper airways near the nose.

SARS-CoV-2 often infects cells in the lower

airways and lungs. This is why people with

COVID-19 can get pneumonia.

FIGHTING BACK

Viruses can be deadly if they keep killing

cells. But the body has ways to fight back.

The immune system protects the body from viruses and other invaders.

One way it does this is with T cells. T cells recognize certain proteins on the surfaces of cells. If the proteins are from the virus, that means the cell is infected. T cells destroy the infected cell. This stops the virus from spreading. However, some viruses

VIRUSES VS. BACTERIA

Viruses and bacteria both cause diseases. But they are very different. Viruses are not alive. They need to take over a cell to reproduce. Bacteria are alive. They make their own energy and reproduce on their own. Viruses cause diseases such as influenza, measles, and COVID-19. Bacteria cause diseases such as tuberculosis and food poisoning.

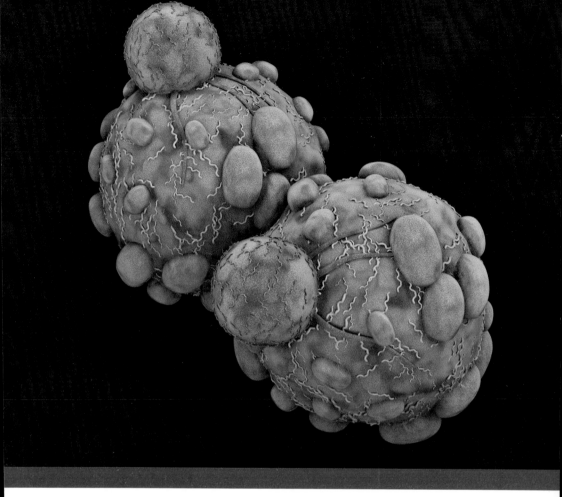

T cells (purple) mark and destroy cells that are infected.

can stop their proteins from appearing on

infected cells. This lets them hide from

T cells. But the immune system is ready

for this too. Natural killer cells notice if a

Antibodies (orange and purple) help other immune cells recognize viruses.

cell has too few proteins on it. They release

chemicals to destroy the cell.

The immune system also uses antibodies

to fight viruses. These are proteins that

recognize viruses and stick to them.

Antibodies may directly stop viruses from infecting cells. They may also cause viruses to stick together. This makes it easier for the immune system to find and destroy the viruses. Antibodies can also trigger certain cells to destroy viruses.

CORONAVIRUSES

There are many kinds of viruses. Coronaviruses form one family of viruses. Their name comes from their appearance. In Latin, *corona* means "crown." Under a microscope, spikes around the edges of the virus make it look like it is wearing a crown.

Some bats carry diseases that can be passed to humans.

Coronaviruses usually infect animals,

such as camels, cats, and bats.

They sometimes infect people too.

Scientists first found human coronaviruses

CORONAVIRUS FEATURES

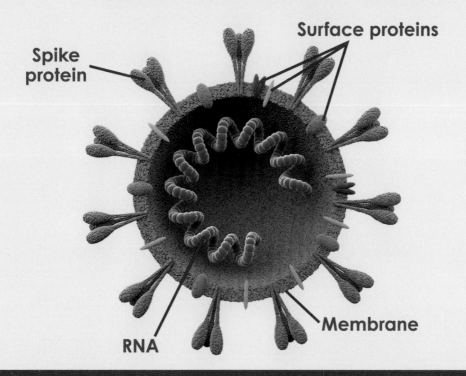

Spike protein

Surface proteins

RNA

Membrane

Proteins on the surface of a coronavirus help it attach to cells. It is able to insert its RNA after attaching.

in the 1960s. Since then, they have discovered a total of seven coronaviruses that infect humans. Four of these cause mild diseases such as colds. Three are more serious.

The first of these is SARS-CoV. It causes Severe Acute **Respiratory** Syndrome (SARS). The *CoV* in the virus's name stands for "coronavirus." Doctors first reported SARS-CoV in China in 2002. The second serious coronavirus is MERS-CoV. It causes Middle East Respiratory Syndrome (MERS). Doctors first saw this virus in 2012 in Saudi

SARS AND MERS

SARS and MERS both had major outbreaks. SARS infected approximately 8,400 people. It killed about 800. There have been only a few minor outbreaks of the disease since 2003. MERS infected approximately 2,500 people but killed more than 850. This gave it a much higher death rate than SARS or COVID-19.

Arabia. The third serious coronavirus is SARS-CoV-2, which causes COVID-19. All three of these diseases can cause severe respiratory problems. However, many SARS-CoV-2 infections are mild. Some people don't even feel sick at all. But for others, the virus is a deadly foe for their immune systems.

STUDYING A NEW VIRUS

When the COVID-19 outbreak began, scientists knew little about the virus. They worked fast to understand how it spread. **Scientific journals** quickly reviewed and published new studies. Researchers joined

Scientists worked together and shared research to learn more about COVID-19.

online discussion groups to share what they

were learning.

Many scientists used preprint servers.

These are places online where researchers

can share studies before they are reviewed

and published. This has positives and negatives. It gets information out as soon as possible. But it also means that bad research may slip through. To many people, this trade-off was worth it. Eric Rubin is the editor in chief of the *New England Journal of Medicine*. He said, "For now, physicians are dealing with a crisis and the best quality information available quickly is better than perfect information that can't be accessed."[1]

CHAPTER TWO

HOW DOES THE VIRUS CAUSE ILLNESS?

When SARS-CoV-2 contacts a human cell, its spikes attach to a protein called ACE2 on the cell. This protein is on many kinds of human cells. But it is especially common in the lungs and intestines.

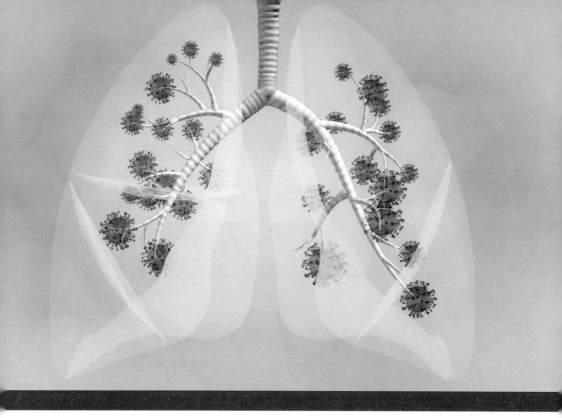

The spiked shape of SARS-CoV-2 helps it attach to cells in the lungs.

SARS-CoV also connects with ACE2. But SARS-CoV-2 is much better at this. It is up to twenty times likelier to attach to the protein. This makes it easier for the virus to infect a cell.

After the virus connects to ACE2, chemical changes take place. These changes let the outer shell of the virus join with the outer layer of the cell. Now, the virus's RNA can get into the cell. It takes over the parts of the cell that usually help the cell reproduce. Instead, these parts build copies of the virus. They can make tens of thousands of new viruses in just a few hours.

The virus also uses this process to create proteins to protect itself. These proteins stop the infected cell from **alerting** the

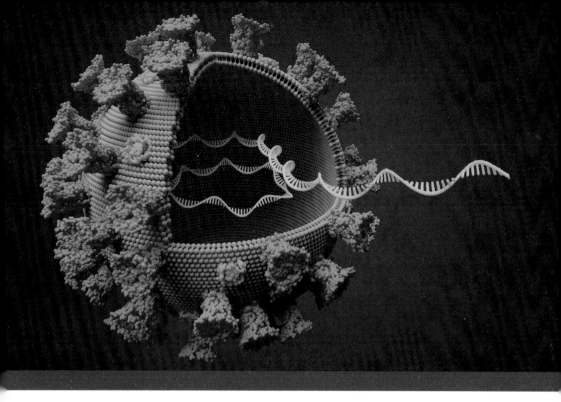

Viruses insert genetic material (yellow) into cells. The cells make more copies of the virus using this material.

immune system. They make the infected

cell release the newly made virus.

IMMUNE RESPONSE

The immune response to SARS-CoV-2

comes in two parts. The first is the innate

response. This begins right after infection. Natural killer cells are one example of innate immune cells. Innate immune cells sense the virus. Then they release proteins called cytokines.

Some cytokines destroy infected cells. This is how natural killer cells work. Other cytokines fight the virus in other ways. For example, one type of cytokine increases body temperature. It causes a fever. Viruses are destroyed at higher temperatures.

Innate immune cells also prepare the second part of the immune response. This is the adaptive response. The innate

The immune system may trigger a fever to destroy invading viruses.

response works against any invader. But the adaptive response is more specific. It targets its response to the specific virus causing the infection.

The adaptive response to SARS-CoV-2 starts six to eight days after infection.

It involves a few different kinds of cells.

Cytotoxic T cells kill the infected cells.

B cells create antibodies to the virus.

And helper T cells activate other kinds of

adaptive immune cells.

Once the infection is gone, the body

needs fewer T and B cells. But some

HOW LONG DOES IMMUNITY LAST?

Immunity to a disease does not necessarily last forever. It varies depending on the disease. People who recover from measles are often immune for life. Scientists worked to discover how long COVID-19 immunity lasts. This is a complex question. There were no clear answers by the fall of 2020.

immune cells are still present. These are memory cells. If the virus comes back in the future, the memory cells will recognize it. They will set off a quick immune response. This may stop the person from getting the disease again.

GETTING SICK

The innate immune response causes the early **symptoms** of COVID-19. Cytokines lead to issues such as fevers and muscle aches. Other early symptoms are a sore throat and a dry cough. As the infection gets worse, the symptoms become more severe. The virus spreads deeper into the

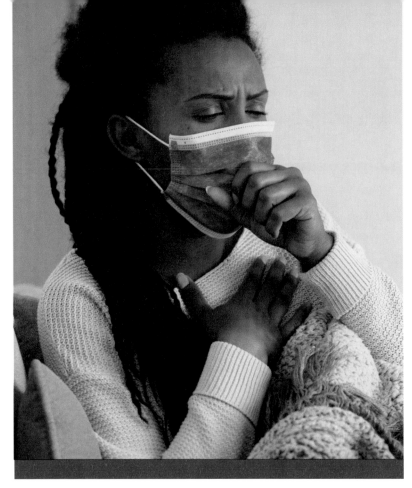

Coughing is a common symptom of COVID-19.

bronchial tubes. These are the passages

leading to the lungs.

Inside the lungs are tiny sacs called

alveoli. When people breathe, oxygen enters

the lungs. The alveoli move this oxygen into

the blood. The bloodstream then carries oxygen throughout the body. Oxygen keeps the body alive and working.

SARS-CoV-2 infects the alveoli. It breaks down the barriers between the alveoli and blood vessels, which allows liquid to leak into the alveoli. This makes breathing harder. The lungs fill with dead cells. The immune system causes **inflammation** in an effort to fight the disease. This damages the lungs even more.

In severe cases, the patient cannot breathe on her own. Doctors must use a machine called a ventilator. The machine pumps air into the person's lungs through a tube in the throat. It breathes for the patient and keeps her alive. But for some people, the damage to the lungs is too severe. Even a ventilator cannot help them. These patients may die from COVID-19.

Lung problems are the most common effects of COVID-19. But the virus can spread elsewhere in the body too. Dr. William Schaffner of Vanderbilt University Medical Center says, "The virus will actually land on organs like the heart, the kidney, the liver, and may cause some direct damage to those organs."[2] As the immune

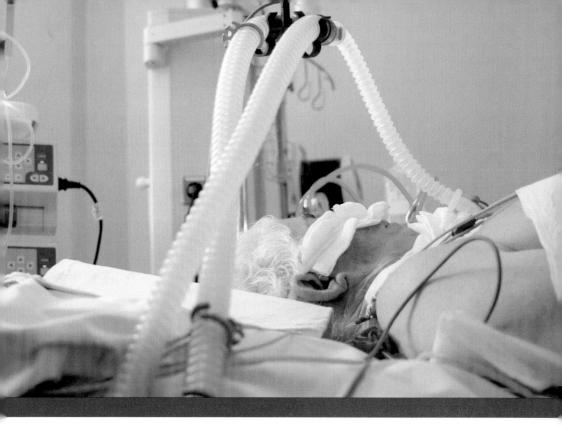

Ventilators help patients with severe cases of COVID-19. These machines provide oxygen.

system battles the virus, it can harm those

organs too.

Symptoms related to the digestive

system have been noted in COVID-19

patients. These include nausea, vomiting,

and diarrhea. People may also lose their

sense of smell or taste. These issues often appear before the respiratory symptoms begin.

VULNERABLE PEOPLE

Older people are at higher risk from COVID-19. Immune cells are made in the bone marrow. As a person ages, the marrow makes fewer cells. This gives the person less defense against the virus. Older people have a higher chance of experiencing severe symptoms.

People with certain health challenges also have a higher risk. This includes those with obesity or diabetes. Their immune systems already produce many cytokines.

An infection will create even more cytokines.

This can make the symptoms of COVID-19

more severe.

CYTOKINE STORMS

Some viruses, including SARS-CoV-2, cause a severe problem called a cytokine storm. In this situation, the immune system releases too many cytokines. Normally, immune suppressor cells stop this harmful immune response. But if those cells are not working, a cytokine storm can happen. The immune cells damage healthy parts of the body. A cytokine storm may kill a patient.

CHAPTER THREE

HOW DOES THE VIRUS SPREAD?

The spread of any virus begins with patient zero. This is the first person to become infected. Finding patient zero can help scientists learn where the disease came from. It can help them prevent future outbreaks.

The way SARS-CoV-2 spreads makes it hard to find patient zero. Some people who

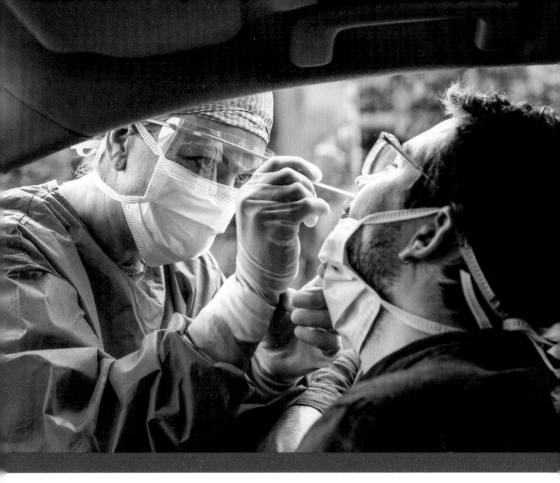

Many cities set up drive-through testing for COVID-19.

are infected are asymptomatic. They do not

show any symptoms. They may not know

they are infected at all. But they can still

spread the virus to others. This means that

many early cases may never be identified.

Scientists believe the virus started in wild animals. This has happened with other coronaviruses. SARS-CoV started in bats. It then infected a palm civet. This is a catlike mammal native to Asia. Finally, the virus jumped to humans at a wet market that sold palm civets. Scientists have long recognized that wet markets can spread disease. Michelle Baker is an **immunologist**. She says, "These wet markets have been identified as an issue because you do have species interacting."[3] After the outbreak of SARS, China banned the sale of palm civets.

Some scientists believe SARS-CoV-2 passed to people from pangolins.

SARS-CoV-2 likely started in bats too. It then infected another animal before spreading to people. Scientists are not sure what this middle animal was. Some believe it was a pangolin. Pangolins are scaly mammals found in Asia and Africa.

People illegally buy them in wet markets for their scales and meat. The virus's genome had clues linking it to pangolins. However, other scientists disagreed with this conclusion. As researchers keep studying the virus, they hope to learn more about where it came from.

MADE BY PEOPLE?

Some people spread rumors about SARS-CoV-2. They said people made the virus in a lab. But scientists found this is false. They studied the virus's genome. They found that the virus came from nature. Human-made viruses are based on existing viruses. But some features of SARS-CoV-2 differ from known viruses. It could not have been formed in a lab.

After the COVID-19 outbreak began, China took dramatic action. It entirely suspended the sale of wildlife. This was a $76 billion industry in the country. The government planned to eventually make the ban permanent.

IN THE AIR

No matter what animal it came from, the virus started spreading. The outbreak quickly grew beyond Wuhan. SARS-CoV-2 reached nearly every country on Earth. Within just a few months, millions of people were infected. The virus spread quickly from person to person.

Travel allowed SARS-CoV-2 to spread quickly around the world. Health officials advised people to limit travel whenever possible.

The main way the virus spreads is through droplets. When a person talks, sings, coughs, or sneezes, tiny droplets come from the mouth and nose. In an infected person, these droplets can contain the virus. The droplets may travel several feet through the air. If another person is nearby, droplets could land in his or her mouth, eyes, or nose. The virus enters the body and may infect the person.

Scientists also found evidence that the virus can spread through aerosols. These are similar to droplets but much smaller. Like droplets, they come from the mouth and nose. But their small size means they can float farther in the air. Aerosols may spread the virus across a wider area. Scientists are still learning how common aerosol spread might be.

SARS-CoV-2 can travel through the air in droplets. People may get sick if these droplets enter their bodies.

This kind of spread can be especially dangerous in places where many people are gathered. Some kinds of places make the spread easier. These include restaurants, nightclubs, and churches.

Places like these are often crowded. People talk, shout, or sing. This sends droplets farther through the air. These places are indoors, and there may not be much fresh air coming in. This makes it easier for droplets to land on people. Major COVID-19

R NAUGHT

One key number in the spread of disease is R0, pronounced "R naught." It is the average number of people one infected person will infect. If a disease's R0 is less than one, the number of infections will go down over time. If the R0 is more than one, the number of infections will grow. Finding the R0 of a new disease is hard, and the number may change over time. In May 2020, scientists estimated the R0 of SARS-CoV-2 to be between 2 and 3.

outbreaks were linked to places like these. One person may infect many others. This is known as a super-spreader event.

ON SURFACES

SARS-CoV-2 can also spread on surfaces. Droplets from an infected person may land on a nearby surface. For example, they may end up on a table or door handle.

Another person might touch that surface. The droplets get on his hands. Then he touches his face. The virus may infect him through his nose, mouth, or eyes. People touch their faces a lot. One study found that it happens more than

Cleaning surfaces with soap or disinfectants destroys SARS-CoV-2.

twenty times per hour. This is one way that

COVID-19 spreads.

Scientists believe that surface spread is

rare compared to spread through the air.

Emanuel Goldman is a professor of biology.

He said, "In my opinion, the chance of

transmission through inanimate surfaces is very small."[4]

STUDYING THE SPREAD

Scientists around the world studied how the virus spreads. One group at the University of Minnesota studied indoor spread. They used a computer program to find out how the virus moves indoors. The computer program showed how air flowed in different rooms.

The researchers tested an elevator, a classroom, and a supermarket. The scientists also showed how ventilation affected the spread. In the classroom test,

Students wore masks to stay safe from the virus at school.

they found that ventilation removed some

aerosols from the air. But many aerosols

stuck to the walls instead. The researchers'

work may help make classrooms and other

indoor spaces safer.

CHAPTER FOUR

WHAT STEPS COULD PEOPLE TAKE TO PROTECT AGAINST THE VIRUS?

The virus spreads easily from person to person. Scientists quickly learned a lot about how COVID-19 spread. As they learned more, they continued to update

Some places required people to take temperature checks before they could enter. Those with fevers who might have COVID-19 were not allowed in.

their advice to the public for how to slow the

spread. This helped save lives. They also

created tests to tell whether people have

COVID-19. This helped treat and control the

disease. Finally, researchers started working

on vaccines. They hoped a vaccine would stop the **pandemic** for good.

STAYING SAFE

The Centers for Disease Control and Prevention (CDC) is a US government agency. Its mission is to protect public health. It provides guidance to the public. The CDC let people know how to stay safe during the pandemic.

One key step was called social distancing. It is sometimes called physical distancing. The CDC defined this as keeping 6 feet (1.8 m) apart from other

Some restaurants offered curbside pickup options. This helped people limit contact with others.

people. That way droplets could not spread from person to person.

Social distancing was important even if both people felt healthy. SARS-CoV-2 can spread before symptoms appear. A person could have COVID-19 and not know it yet. It was safest to stay apart.

Social distancing affected daily life. People were careful on buses or trains. They picked distanced seats if possible. They used curbside pickup or delivery service if possible. Hanging out with friends could be done online instead of in person. People could video chat or play online games together.

Another key step to protect people was to wear a mask. Masks should cover the mouth and nose. This stops droplets from leaving a person and infecting others. Masks were one of the simplest and most effective ways to stop the spread.

Masks prevent droplets from spreading through the air.

Dr. Robert Redfield, the head of the CDC, talked about masks in September 2020. He said, "These face masks are the most important powerful public health tool we have."[5]

The CDC offered tips on using masks. It recommended that masks have at least two layers of fabric. The user should be able to breathe easily through it. The mask should have a tight fit on the sides of the face. There should be no air gaps. These can let the virus escape into the air.

The third key step to slow the spread was handwashing. Health experts

HEALTH CARE WORKERS

Health care workers were in close contact with COVID-19 patients during the pandemic. They used extra protective gear to stay safe. These workers wore N95 masks. Like cloth masks, they stop droplets from leaving the nose and mouth. But they can also stop the virus from getting in. Health care workers also wore gloves and gowns. They used goggles or face shields to help protect their eyes.

recommended people wash with soap and warm water for at least twenty seconds. People should wash after touching surfaces or being near people who may be infected. Soap breaks up the outer layer of SARS-CoV-2 and destroys the virus. Washing for twenty seconds is enough time for this to happen.

Dr. Daniel Pastula is a disease expert at UCHealth in Colorado. He said any kind of soap will work. "It can be fancy mall soap. It can be 50-cent generic unscented soap. . . . All soaps work the same.

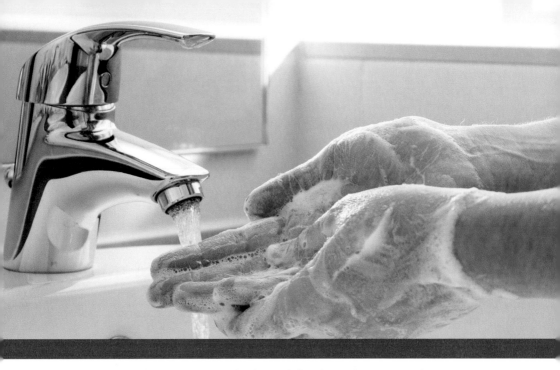

Soap destroys SARS-CoV-2 before it can enter the body.

And soap doesn't only work for this virus. It works on many other viruses and bacteria."[6]

TESTING

Social distancing, masks, and handwashing helped prevent the spread. But it was also important to track the virus when it did spread. This was done by testing. Scientists developed two basic types of testing for COVID-19. The first was diagnostic testing. The second was antibody testing.

Diagnostic tests show if a person currently has the disease. There are two kinds of diagnostic tests. Molecular tests look for the virus's genetic material. Antigen tests look for proteins that are on the surface of the virus. Both kinds usually use a cotton swab to collect mucus from the nose or throat. Molecular results may come back the same day. Antigen results may be available within an hour. However, wait times were often longer during the worst of the pandemic. Labs were overwhelmed with tests. Some people had to wait a week or even longer for results.

Antibody tests look for the antibodies that the immune system makes against SARS-CoV-2. They cannot be used to find an active infection. But they can show who has already had COVID-19. Antibody tests use a blood sample. The results may come back the same day, though it may take longer if labs are busy.

Both kinds of tests are useful. With diagnostic tests, people who test positive can get quick medical care. They can

A cotton swab is used to collect mucus for COVID-19 testing.

contact people they have seen recently.

Those people can get tested and stay

away from others. These steps can slow

the disease's spread. With antibody tests,

scientists can track how far the disease has

spread. The tests reveal who has had the

Experts advised people who were exposed to the virus to get tested and stay at home.

virus, even if they did not show symptoms.

Knowing about the spread helped experts

and leaders plan a response.

It's important to remember that no test

is 100 percent accurate. A test may return

a false negative. This means the person

actually has the virus, but the test says she does not. In rare cases, a test may return a false positive. This means the person does not have the virus, but the test says she does. During the pandemic, scientists continued to work on improving tests.

VACCINE

Scientists knew a vaccine would be the best way to bring an end to the pandemic. Vaccines are medicines that prevent diseases. They prepare the immune system to fight a certain disease. Past vaccines have eliminated dangerous diseases such as polio and smallpox.

At the beginning of the pandemic, there was no vaccine for COVID-19. The virus had only recently been discovered. Scientists raced to create a vaccine. Vaccines usually take years to create. But COVID-19 was an especially deadly disease. Making a vaccine quickly could save lives.

Vaccines must go through testing before they can be given to the public. These tests make sure the vaccine works against the disease. They also make sure the vaccine is safe for people to take.

There are several steps in the testing process. First, scientists test a vaccine

Scientists around the world worked to develop a COVID-19 vaccine.

on animals. They watch how the animals'
immune systems react. Next are phase
one trials. A small group of people get the
vaccine. Scientists watch for any bad side
effects. They also see how the human
immune system reacts. During phase two

trials, hundreds of people get the vaccine. They are split into groups, such as younger and older. Scientists see if the vaccine affects the groups differently. They continue to watch for safety issues. The next step is phase three trials. Thousands of people get the vaccine. Scientists compare these people to those who did not get a vaccine. This will show how well the vaccine actually works. These large tests can also find rare side effects.

If phase three trials go well, the vaccine may be approved for the public. The first COVID-19 vaccine trials began in March

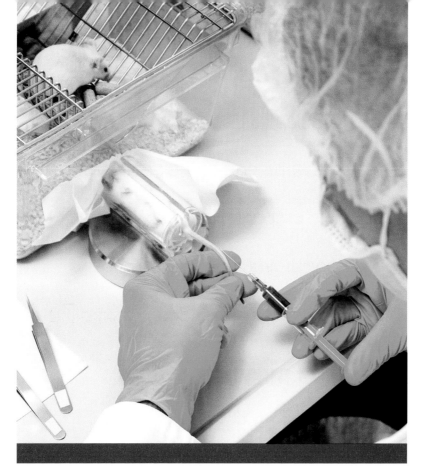

Vaccines may be tested on animals such as mice before they are used on people.

2020. By November, thirteen vaccines were in phase three. Two companies released early results that showed their vaccines were more than 90 percent effective. Many more vaccines were in phases one and two. Scientists hoped to get a vaccine approved by the end of the year. Drug companies prepared to create millions of doses of approved vaccines and send them all over the world.

DEFEATING THE VIRUS

SARS-CoV-2 changed the world. It affected daily life for people in almost every country. It sickened tens of millions. And it killed more than 1 million people.

Scientists led the fight against the deadly virus. They decoded its genome. They learned how it spreads and makes people sick. They figured out ways to test for it.

They gave advice on how to protect against it. And they raced to create a vaccine. By studying SARS-CoV-2, scientists saved lives and learned new information that would help bring the pandemic to an end.

OPERATION WARP SPEED

In April 2020, the US government announced Operation Warp Speed. This program was designed to speed up the making of a vaccine. The government provided almost $10 billion. Some money went to research. Other money helped companies prepare to produce and distribute vaccine doses. The goal of Operation Warp Speed was to start delivering 300 million doses of effective vaccines in January 2021.

GLOSSARY

alerting
sending a warning about something

immunologist
a scientist who studies the immune system

invade
to enter a place or an object

pandemic
an outbreak of disease that occurs over a wide area

proteins
chemicals that are the building blocks of living things

reproduce
to create offspring or copies of a living thing

respiratory
related to the process of breathing

scientific journals
publications that print scientific research papers

symptoms
the effects that a person feels from a disease

SOURCE NOTES

CHAPTER ONE: WHAT IS A CORONAVIRUS?

1. Quoted in Kai Kupferschmidt, "'A Completely New Culture of Doing Research.' Coronavirus Outbreak Changes How Scientists Communicate," *Science*, February 26, 2020. www.sciencemag.org.

CHAPTER TWO: HOW DOES THE VIRUS CAUSE ILLNESS?

2. Quoted in Pam Belluck, "What Does the Coronavirus Do to the Body?" *New York Times*, March 26, 2020. www.nytimes.com.

CHAPTER THREE: HOW DOES THE VIRUS SPREAD?

3. Quoted in Graham Readfearn, "How Did Coronavirus Start and Where Did It Come From? Was It Really Wuhan's Animal Market?" *Guardian*, April 27, 2020. www.theguardian.com.

4. Quoted in Stephanie Watson, "Coronavirus on Surfaces: What's the Real Risk?" *WebMD*, September 3, 2020. www.webmd.com.

CHAPTER FOUR: WHAT STEPS COULD PEOPLE TAKE TO PROTECT AGAINST THE VIRUS?

5. Quoted in Caitlin O'Kane, "CDC Director Says Face Masks May Offer More Protection Against COVID than a Vaccine. Here's What Other Experts Say," *CBS News*, September 18, 2020. www.cbsnews.com.

6. Quoted in Katie Kerwin McCrimmon, "Why Soap and Water Work Better than Hand Sanitizer to Remove the Coronavirus," *UCHealth*, March 30, 2020. www.uchealth.org.

FOR FURTHER RESEARCH

BOOKS

Renae Giles, *The Science of the Coronavirus*. Minneapolis, MN: Lerner, 2020.

Douglas Hustad, *Understanding COVID-19*. Minneapolis, MN: Abdo, 2020.

Alexis Roumanis, *Explaining the COVID-19 Pandemic*. Vancouver, British Columbia, Canada: Engage Books, 2020.

INTERNET SOURCES

"Coronavirus Disease (COVID-19) Advice for the Public: Mythbusters," *WHO*, 2020. www.who.int.

"COVID-19 Resource and Information Guide," *NAMI*, 2020. www.nami.org.

"How COVID-19 Spreads," *CDC*, October 28, 2020. www.cdc.gov.

WEBSITES

Coronavirus.gov
www.coronavirus.gov

Coronavirus.gov is the US government's official dashboard for information related to the COVID-19 pandemic.

Johns Hopkins COVID-19 Dashboard
https://coronavirus.jhu.edu/map

The Johns Hopkins COVID-19 dashboard provides global information on the COVID-19 pandemic.

WHO Coronavirus Disease (COVID-19) Dashboard
https://covid19.who.int/

The World Health Organization (WHO) dashboard provides global information on the COVID-19 pandemic.

INDEX

IMAGE CREDITS

ABOUT THE AUTHOR

Walt K. Moon is a writer who lives in Minnesota. He enjoys learning and reading about all kinds of science, including the science of public health.